MY SCIENCE BOOK OF MACHINES

Written by
Neil Ardley

DK

Dorling Kindersley
London • New York • Stuttgart

What are machines?

Machines are inventions that do jobs for us. Some are small and simple, like a bottle opener or a pair of scissors. Others are large and complicated, like trains and cranes. Machines can help us do a job faster or make it easier. They can lift or move things, and do jobs we could not do by ourselves. Some machines use our own muscle power to work, but others have powerful engines or motors.

Do the locomotion
Steam locomotives were the first machines to make quick, long-distance travel possible.

Canny device
This machine opens cans easily and safely. When you grip and turn the handles, the blade is forced into the lid and slices it open.

Get a lift
You can lift a car all by yourself, if you use a jack. The parts inside the jack move so that it pushes upwards. It pushes with much more strength than you use to turn the handle.

A Dorling Kindersley Book

Project Editors Scott Steedman and Laura Buller
Art Editors Mark Regardsoe and Earl Neish
Production Louise Barratt
Photography Dave King

First published in Great Britain in 1992 by Dorling
Kindersley Publishers Limited, 9 Henrietta Street,
London WC2E 8PS

British Library Cataloguing in Publication Data is available

ISBN 0-86318-685-8

Reproduced in Hong Kong by Bright Arts
Printed in Belgium by Proost

Smart machine
All you have to do to make this washing machine do the washing is switch it on. It is automatic – it works under its own control.

Speedy sums
When you press the buttons of this calculator, electricity moves through the parts inside it, and it does sums very quickly.

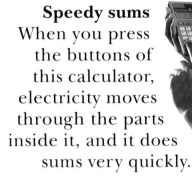

Non-stop workers
Robots are machines that can be "taught" to copy human movements, and do jobs which people find boring or dangerous. Other machines, such as paint sprayers or welding torches, can be worked by robots.

⚠ This sign means **take care**. You should ask an adult to help you with this step of the experiment.

Be a safe scientist
Follow all the directions carefully and always take care, especially with glass, scissors, matches, candles, and electricity.

Never put anything in your mouth or eyes. Treat the machines you make with care. They may hurt you or others if you try to make them work too fast or hard.

Load lifter

Machines can give you more strength! Build a wheelbarrow and move a heavy load of stones. It works with a "lever". A lever lets you move things with less effort.

You will need:

Stones

Two equal lengths of wood

Short pencil

Sticky tape

Card

Shoe box

Cotton reel

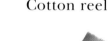
Plastic bag

Scissors

1 Put the stones into the bag and lift them. It takes a lot of effort!

2 Tape the card inside the box to make two sections.

Angle the lengths of wood slightly.

The cotton reel should just fit between these ends.

3 Tape the lengths of wood firmly to the bottom of the box.

4 Stick the pencil through the cotton reel and tape it between the lengths of wood. This is your wheelbarrow.

5 Put the bag of stones in the back section of the wheelbarrow. Now it is easy to lift and move the heavy load of stones!

The lever tilts around the wheel.

The lengths of wood form a lever. The effort of your hands raises the end of the lever.

You use less effort when the load is nearer to the wheel.

6 Move the bag of stones to the front section. This time, it is much easier to lift the heavy load.

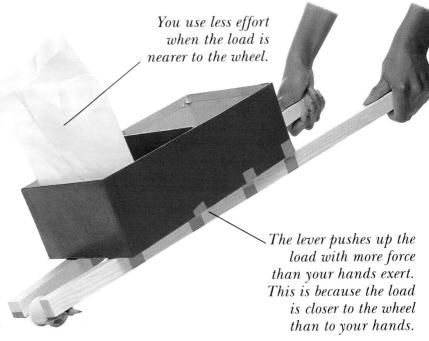

The lever pushes up the load with more force than your hands exert. This is because the load is closer to the wheel than to your hands.

Strong-arm tactic
A spanner gives you the strength to fasten a bolt. It works as a lever. The movement you make to turn the handle becomes a shorter but more powerful movement at the other end.

Raising the rice

You can lift some cereal out of a bowl with the help of a lifting machine called an "auger". An auger uses a screw to raise things up a tube.

You will need:

Wooden rod

Bowl of puffed rice

Small bowl

Pen

Sticky tape

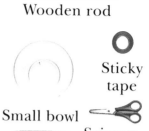

Scissors

Narrow plastic bottle

Card

1 ⚠ Ask an adult to cut off both ends of the bottle to make a tube slightly shorter than the rod.

2 Using one end of the tube, draw six circles on the card.

3 Draw a small circle in the centre of each circle. Cut out the larger circles. Then cut across to the small ones and cut them out.

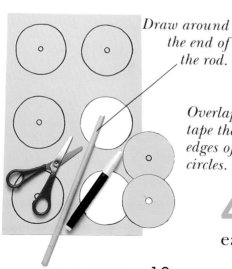

Draw around the end of the rod.

Overlap and tape the cut edges of the circles.

4 Tape the circles together, each one on top of the next.

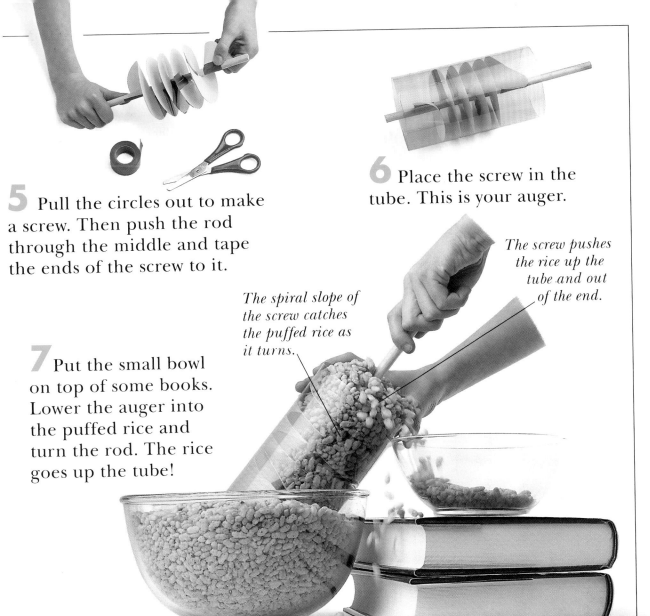

5 Pull the circles out to make a screw. Then push the rod through the middle and tape the ends of the screw to it.

6 Place the screw in the tube. This is your auger.

The screw pushes the rice up the tube and out of the end.

The spiral slope of the screw catches the puffed rice as it turns.

7 Put the small bowl on top of some books. Lower the auger into the puffed rice and turn the rod. The rice goes up the tube!

Gathering the grain
A combine harvester cuts wheat and removes grain at the same time. Inside it are several augers. One moves the cut stalks. Others move the loose grain up a chute and into a waiting trailer.

Sort it out

Build a machine that sorts large marbles from small ones. It is an "automatic" machine, which means it works under its own control. Make sure the boxes you use for this are all the same height.

You will need:

Straw

Kebab stick

Two short cardboard boxes

Glue

Large and sma
pieces of card

One long cardboard box

Big and small marbles

Tape

Scissors

Plasticine

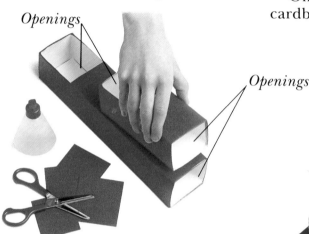
Openings

Openings

1 Cut openings in the long box and in one of the short boxes. Glue them together.

To make a channel, fold the card down against the edge of a table, then fold it back.

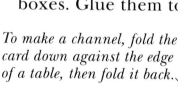

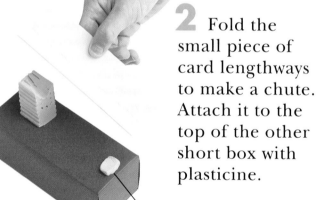

2 Fold the small piece of card lengthways to make a chute. Attach it to the top of the other short box with plasticine.

Use a small piece of plasticine on this end.

3 Make a channel on each side of the large piece of card. Turn it over, and tape the straw to the middle of the card. Put the stick through the straw.

12

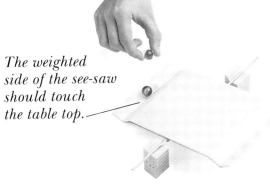

The weighted side of the see-saw should touch the table top.

4 Stick two small marbles into one of the channels with plasticine. Balance the stick on two blocks of plasticine. This is your see-saw.

The see-saw must line up with the bottom of the top box.

5 Line up the boxes, see-saw, and chute. Roll a small marble down the chute. It goes into the upper box.

A small marble is not heavy enough to tilt the see-saw.

Add more plasticine if the chute does not line up with the see-saw and boxes.

Big marbles are heavy enough to tilt the see-saw.

6 Roll a heavy marble down the chute. The see-saw tilts, and the marble goes into the lower box.

Mail machine
Letters and parcels go through automatic sorting machines that detect post codes and sort all the mail for each post code together.

Wind and whirl

How can you turn one reel and cause four to spin? By using a belt, you will see how some machines carry motion from one moving part to another.

You will need:

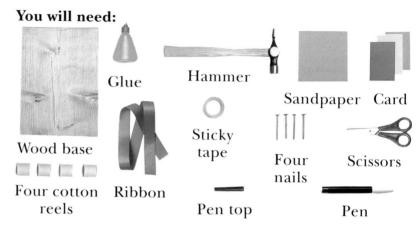

Wood base

Glue

Hammer

Sandpaper   Card

Sticky tape

Four nails

Scissors

Four cotton reels   Ribbon

Pen top   Pen

1 Cut four strips of sandpaper and glue them around the four reels.

2 Arrange the cotton reels on the base as shown.

Each reel should turn easily.

3 ⚠ Ask an adult to hammer a nail through the centre hole of each reel.

4 Loop the ribbon around the reels. Pull it tight and tape it together. Push the pen top into the top reel.

6 Push the arrows into the three bottom reels.

5 Draw an arrow on each card and cut them out.

7 Using the pen top as a handle, turn the top reel. The three arrows whirl round.

The ribbon is a belt. Turning the handle moves the belt, making all the reels turn.

The middle arrow whirls in the opposite direction to the other two arrows.

Round and round
Beating eggs is easy with this machine. When the handle is turned, the motion is transferred to two wheels. These wheels whirl the beaters in opposite directions so that they beat the eggs well.

Jump for joy

Make a figure jump up and down by turning a handle. You can do this with a machine that changes circular motion into an up-and-down movement.

You will need:

Round lid

Sticky tape

Scissors

Shoe box with lid

Straw

Card

Pliers

Pen

Metal knitting need

Thin stick

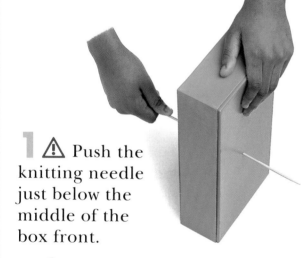

1 ⚠ Push the knitting needle just below the middle of the box front.

2 ⚠ Ask an adult to bend the sharp end of the knitting needle. Tape it to the inside of the round lid.

Place the bend against the bottom edge of the lid.

Rotate the lid to its highest position.

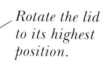

3 ⚠ Ask an adult to bend the other end of the knitting needle to form a handle.

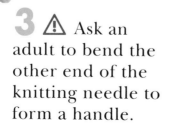

4 Cut a short piece of straw. Then tape it to the box above the lid

16

5 Draw a figure on the card. Cut it out and tape it to the stick.

6 Drop the stick into the straw so that the end rests on the round lid.

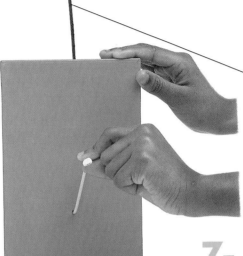

As it turns, the lid pushes the stick up through the straw and then lets it fall.

7 Turn the handle. The figure jumps up and down!

Engine power
This old engine changes one kind of movement to another. Powerful jets of steam drive a long rod back and forth. Links called cranks connect the rod to the wheels. The cranks change the back-and-forth movement of the rod to make the wheels turn round.

Keeping cool

Keep cool with a hand-powered fan. This machine uses a "gear". The gear makes the fan spin faster than the handle you are turning. Gears allow parts of machines to work at different speeds.

You will need:

Thin wooden stick

Drawing pin

Paper fastener

Three corks

Hammer

Box

Plastic

Rubber band

Knife

Scissors

Nail

Jar lid

Put the holes about 5cm from the top and bottom of the box.

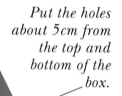

2 Push the drawing pin through the hole in the side of the lid. Stick a cork on to the pin. This is the handle.

Put one hole in the middle of the lid and another hole towards the edge.

1 ⚠ Ask an adult to make two holes in the front of the box. Turn the box over and make a hole opposite one of the holes. Then make two holes in the jar lid.

The handle should turn easily.

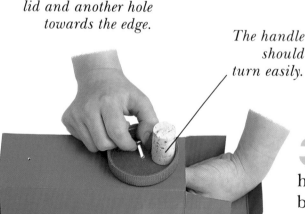

3 Attach the handle to the box with the paper fastener.

*Make the
slits slant
a little.*

4 ⚠ Ask an adult
to cut four evenly
spaced slits in one
of the corks.

5 Cut four long strips from the
plastic. Each one should be as
wide as the slits in the cork.

*The stick should
be long enough
to come out of
the other side
of the box.*

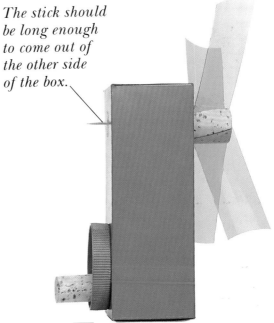

6 ⚠ Push the strips into the
slits in the cork to form the
blades of the fan. Push one end
of the stick into the cork.

7 Push the stick through
the other two holes in the
box as shown.

Continued on next page

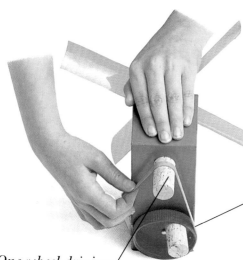

8 Push the other cork on to the uncovered end of the stick. Loop the rubber band around the cork and jar lid. This is your fan.

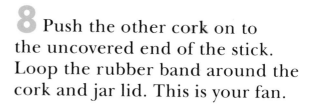

The rubber band should fit without much stretching.

One wheel driving another is called a gear. Here, a belt (the rubber band) links the two wheels (the lid and cork).

The blades spin faster than the handle turns, because the jar lid is a bigger wheel than the cork that it drives.

9 Wind the handle of the fan. The blades spin rapidly and blow air forward!

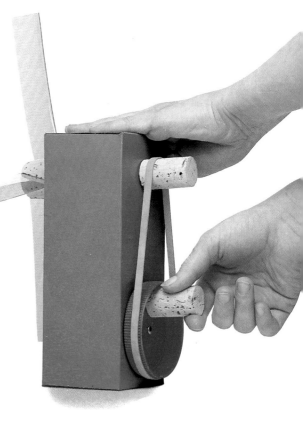

Speedy ride

Gears help you to pedal a bicycle. The chain drives toothed gears on the back wheel. The smaller gears turn the wheel many times for each turn of the pedal.

Continued from previous page

Ball bearing

Parts of machines can rub together as they move. The rubbing, called "friction", slows machines down. Make a ball bearing and see how it reduces friction.

You will need:

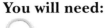

Scissors

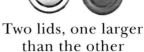
Two lids, one larger than the other

Plasticine

Marbles

Pencil

Sticky tape

1 Stick the small lid to a table top. Tape the pencil across the large lid.

2 Place the large lid over the small lid and spin it. The top lid hardly moves.

Friction between the lids stops them from spinning well.

The marbles should roll easily and keep the lids apart.

The rolling marbles reduce the friction.

3 Now put some marbles inside the small lid.

4 Replace the large lid and spin it again. This time, the lid spins easily.

Reel racer

Some machines have motors to give them power. You can make a rubber band motor to power a cotton reel. It provides enough force to drive the reel at high speed!

You will need:

Cork

Five rubber bands

Metal knitting needle

Used match

Sticky tape

Plastic bottle cap

Cotton reel

Scissors

1 Wind four of the rubber bands around the cotton reel to make two tyres.

2 Thread the fifth band through the centre of the reel. Push the match through the end of the rubber band and tape it to the reel.

3 ⚠ Ask an adult to make a hole in the bottle cap.

The rubber band should be tight. Knot the band if it is too long.

4 Push the other end of the rubber band through the hole in the cap. Slip the knitting needle through the rubber band.

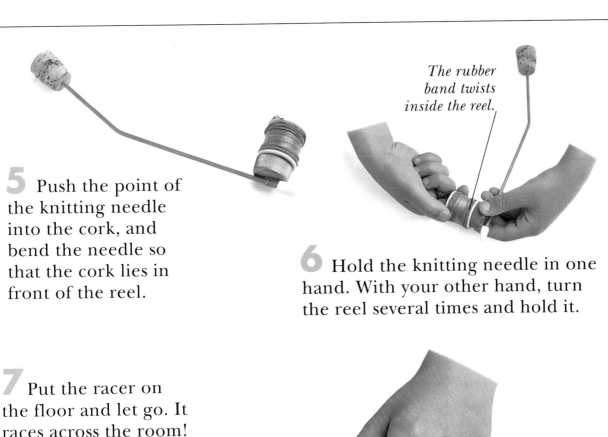

The rubber band twists inside the reel.

5 Push the point of the knitting needle into the cork, and bend the needle so that the cork lies in front of the reel.

6 Hold the knitting needle in one hand. With your other hand, turn the reel several times and hold it.

7 Put the racer on the floor and let go. It races across the room! You could make two reels and race them.

As the rubber band untwists, it produces a force that turns the reel and drives the racer forward.

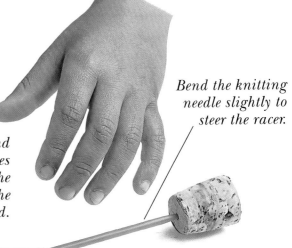

Bend the knitting needle slightly to steer the racer.

Driving force
This motorcycle changes the power provided by an engine into movement. The engine turns a rod that is attached by a chain to the back wheel. The wheel turns with enough force to push the motorcycle forward.

Water works

Raise a heavy weight – with just a little water! Build your own "hydraulic" machine. It uses liquid to force things to move.

You will need:

Rubber band
Plastic tube
Sticky tape
Book

Plastic bottle
Balloon
Water
Scissors
Funnel
Can

1 Put the balloon over the tube and secure with a rubber band. Make a tight seal with tape.

2 ⚠ Ask an adult to cut the top off the plastic bottle, and to cut a hole in the side, near the base.

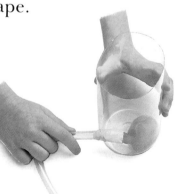

3 Push the balloon through the hole in the bottle.

4 Tape the funnel to the end of the tube.

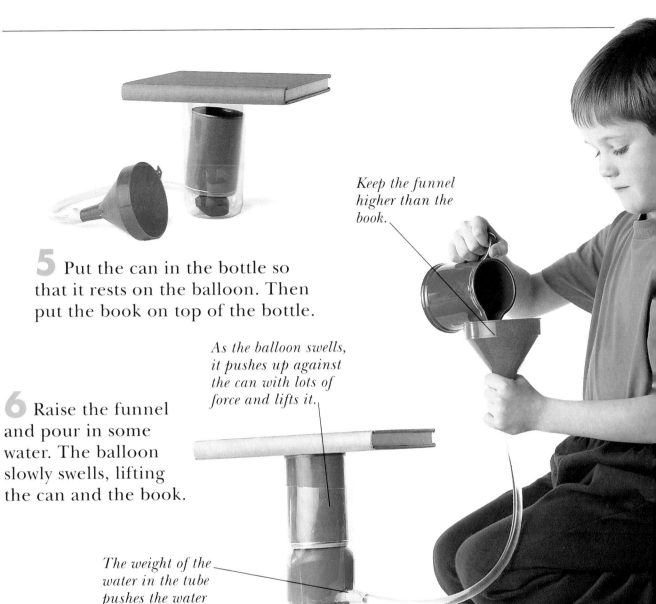

5 Put the can in the bottle so that it rests on the balloon. Then put the book on top of the bottle.

Keep the funnel higher than the book.

As the balloon swells, it pushes up against the can with lots of force and lifts it.

6 Raise the funnel and pour in some water. The balloon slowly swells, lifting the can and the book.

The weight of the water in the tube pushes the water into the balloon.

Big digger

Powerful excavators use hydraulics. Pipes carry liquid from a pump to cylinders, where it pushes out pistons with great force. The pistons drive the bucket into the ground and raise a heavy load of soil.

Pulley power

Pulling something downwards is easier than lifting it up. A "pulley" changes a downward pull into an upward lift. You can build a model crane that uses a pulley to lift a load.

You will need:

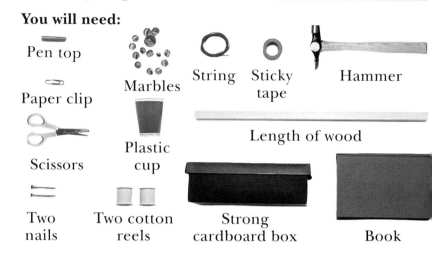

Pen top

Paper clip

Scissors

Two nails

Marbles

Plastic cup

Two cotton reels

String

Sticky tape

Hammer

Length of wood

Strong cardboard box

Book

Hammer

Position the reels on the wood as shown.

1 ⚠ Ask an adult to nail the two reels to the wood. The reels should be able to turn easily.

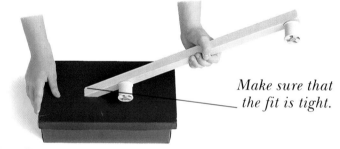

Make sure that the fit is tight.

2 Cut a hole in the box. Insert the wood so that it sticks out at an angle.

3 Cut a short piece of string. Then tape the ends to the cup like the handle on a bucket.

4 Push the pen top into the lower reel to form a handle. Tape one end of the remaining string to this reel.

6 Bend the paper clip to make a hook. Tie it to the end of the string.

5 Loop the string over the top reel. Then hold the string tight while you wind it on to the bottom reel.

Place a book on the box. This is a "counterweight". It stops the load from pulling the crane over.

The upper reel is a pulley wheel. It changes the downward force of the handle into an upward force that lifts the load.

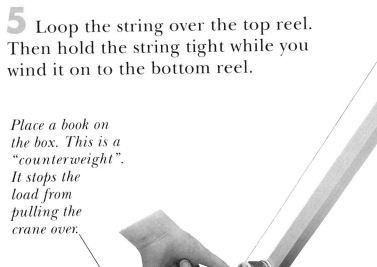

7 Fill the cup with marbles and hook it to the crane. Then wind the handle to lift the cup.

High-rise machine
A tower crane has a long arm called a jib that lowers a hook to the load. As the crane raises or lowers the load, the jib swivels round to move the load sideways. A huge counterweight at the other end of the jib stops the crane from toppling over.

Superkid

Make yourself super-strong with a special pulley. Use it to pull two people together, even though they struggle to stay apart!

You will need:

Two broom handles

Long piece of rope

1 Ask a friend to hold a broom handle with both hands. Then tie the rope to it.

2 Ask another friend to hold the other handle, opposite your first friend.

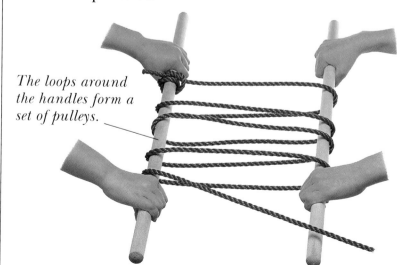

The loops around the handles form a set of pulleys.

3 Loop the rope around the broom handles several times.

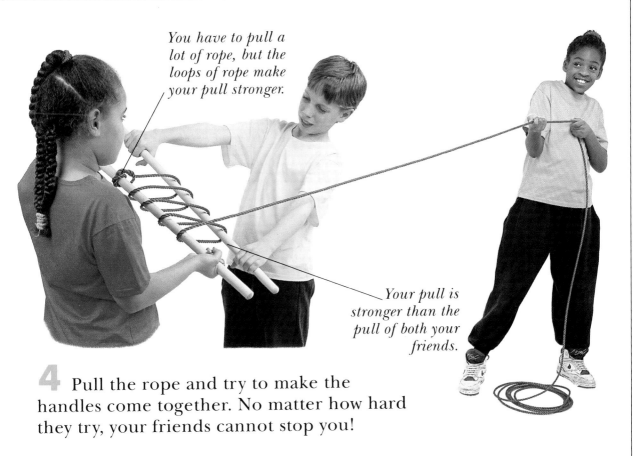

You have to pull a lot of rope, but the loops of rope make your pull stronger.

Your pull is stronger than the pull of both your friends.

4 Pull the rope and try to make the handles come together. No matter how hard they try, your friends cannot stop you!

Pulling power

The set of pulleys hanging from this crane is called a block and tackle. One rope passes around the pulleys. The block and tackle can lift a heavy load with just a light pull on the rope.

Picture credits
(Picture credits abbreviation key: B=below, C=centre, L=left, R=right, T=top)

Robert Harding Picture Library/Ian Griffiths: 23BL; Christopher D. Howson: 6BL; The Image Bank: 11BL, 13BL;/Al Satterwhite: 25BR;/Jurgen Voight: 27BL; Pictor International: 17BL;

Science Photo Library/David Parker/ 600 Group: 7C; Tony Stone Worldwide/ Jon Riley: 29C; Zefa Picture Library: 7TL;/M. Mehltretter: 6TL.

Picture research Kathy Lockley and Clive Webster

Science consultant Jack Challoner

Dorling Kindersley would like to thank Jenny Vaughan for editorial assistance; Mrs Bradbury, Mr Millington, the staff and children of Allfarthing Junior School, Wandsworth, especially Daniel Armstrong, Gemma Bradford, Lucy Gibson, Keisha McLeod, Kate Miller, Sonia Opong, Ben Sells, Cheryl Small, Ruth Tross, Duncan Warren; Kate Ling, Lori Randall, Luke Randall; and Kristy Gould.